halloween parties

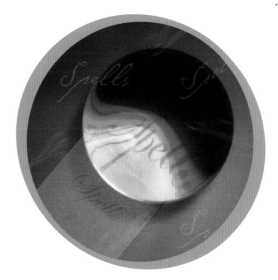

halloween parties

HOW TO THROW SPOOK-TACULAR SOIREES
& FRIGHTENINGLY FESTIVE ENTERTAINMENTS

LORI HELLANDER

Photographs by Bill Milne

STEWART, TABORI & CHANG
New York

Prairie Trails Public Library

Published by
STEWART, TABORI & CHANG
115 West 18th Street
New York, NY 10011

Canadian Distribution:
Canadian Manda Group
One Atlantic Avenue, Suite 105
Toronto, Ontario M6K 3E7
Canada

Quirk Packaging, Inc.
119 W 23rd St., Suite 1001
New York, NY 10011

Library of Congress Cataloging-in-Publication Data

Hellander, Lori.
    Halloween Parties : how to throw spook-tacular soirees and frighteningly festive entertainments / Lori Hellander ; photographs by Bill Milne.
        p. cm.
    ISBN 1-58479-339-2
    1. Halloween cookery. 2. Parties. I. Title.

 TX739.2.H34H45 2004
 641.5'68–dc22
                                2004041658

The text of this book was composed in Rabbit Ears, Bell Gothic, and Sabon.
Design by Lynne Yeamans and Christine Licata

Printed in China

10 9 8 7 6 5 4 3 2 1

First Printing

Stewart, Tabori & Chang is a subsidiary of

contents

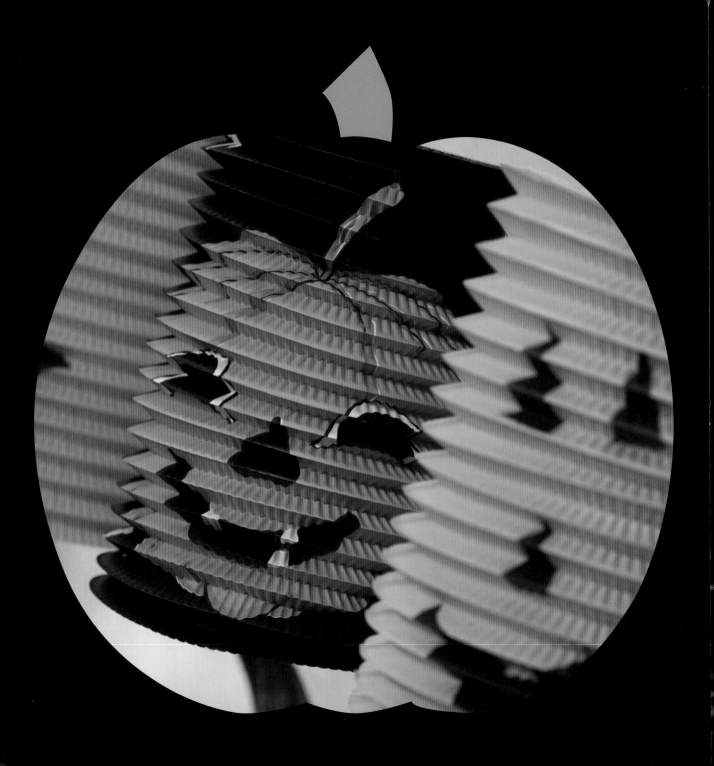

introduction

HALLOWEEN: a frightfully good night (or day) for a party!

are you a halloween enthusiast?

TAKE THIS QUIZ AND FIND OUT:

true or false:

1 Halloween is not just for kids

2 Halloween is not merely a night, but a season

3 The right day to start planning next year's costume is November 1

4 Everyone should own a collection of specialized pumpkin-carving tools

5 You can never have too much candy

If you answered "True" to even one of these statements, you are a true Halloween devotee—and you know that there is no better occasion for a party. This book is dedicated to helping you to throw a thoroughly thrilling Halloween celebration—every year!

Here are six stylishly spook-tacular party plans sure to send delightful shivers through Halloween hosts and their guests. Themes range from the traditional (Tricks & Treats) to the offbeat (It's a Mod, Mod World!), and each one offers plenty of room for improvisation. You can invite everyone you know to a big bash or host an intimate get-together for only your closest pals, plan a sophisticated soiree for grown-up guests or a lively celebration for Halloween-lovers of all ages. For each fest, you'll find a sample invitation, decorating ideas, party favors, entertainment suggestions, and recipes for food and drink. Some parties can be thrown together in a flash, others will require a bit of preparation—and each one can be modified to suit your schedule and budget.

Whether your idea of a great Halloween event is a spine-tingling scarefest, a nostalgic costume party, or a pumpkin-carving extravaganza, you'll find lots of inspiration in these pages to enjoy a frightfully good Halloween.

tricks &
treats

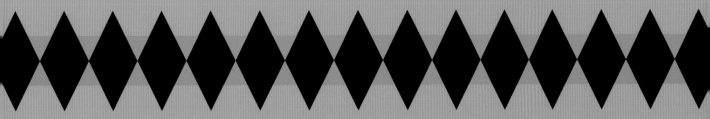

ARE YOU MISSING THE DAYS WHEN YOU GOT TO DRESS AS A PIRATE, clown, or fairy princess and go out trick-or-treating? This party recaptures all the childhood pleasures of Halloween—dress up in your favorite costume, eat too much candy, carve a crazy pumpkin; and because it's a party for grown-ups, you can also enjoy mulled wine and cider.

costume party

WHIP UP THIS CLEVER INVITATION using decorative papers combined with clipart images, photos of Halloweens past, or vintage photos of kids in costume. Complete your handiwork with a witty poem and encourage your guest to fill in the blank with his or her intended disguise.

Come to a party on Halloween,
Dream up a costume
    in which to be seen.
Let your imagination go wild,
Call upon your inner child:

"I wish I may,
I wish I might
Be _____
    for just tonight!"

PARTY October 31
TIME 9 p.m. to ?
PLACE 10 Candy Avenue
    (insert your address here)
BRING Your imagination and
    a favorite childhood photo
    of you in costume.

YOU'LL NEED:
Halloween-themed photo or clipart to photocopy
Scissors
Glue
Decorative paper of your choice
Envelopes to fit the finished invitations

1 Cut out the photo or clipart image you'd like to use and paste it to a piece of decorative paper.

2 Using a color copier, make as many copies as you need. Make sure they are the right size to fit your envelopes.

3 Print the invitation text directly onto the back of the color copies using your computer printer or, if you're feeling calligraphic, hand-letter the text onto each invitation.

pumpkin pointers

- **THE SHAPE OF THINGS TO CARVE:** Choose pumpkins with flat bottoms, smooth contours, and pleasing stems.

- **ORANGE SMOOTHIE:** Pumpkins shrivel because they lose moisture after they've been carved. To keep your Jack wrinkle-free for as long as possible, coat all cut surfaces with a thin layer of petroleum jelly or vegetable oil.

jack-o'-lantern goody bags

THESE FUN FAVORS GIVE YOUR GUESTS EVERYTHING THEY NEED to decorate a gourd that's as groovy or gooney as they choose. Prepare a tableful of carving tools for everyone to share, and give each guest a goody bag of decorations for dressing up a pumpkin in style.

YOU'LL NEED:
Small black gift bags
Halloween ribbons
Crepe paper or cut-out paper pumpkin
Crinkle paper
Gag gift (a can of silly string
   or wax lips, for example)

FOR THE PUMPKIN-DECORATING:
Hot glue gun and plenty
   of glue sticks
Sequins, large and small
Sequin pins
Glitter
Markers

1 Remove the handles from the gift bags and replace them with Halloween ribbons. Attach a paper pumpkin ornament to the front of the bag.

2 Fill the bag with crinkle paper, supplies for decorating the pumpkin, and the little gag gift "trick."

playing with pumpkins

AMONG THE MOST CHARMING ASPECTS OF PUMPKINS ARE THEIR PLEASANT NAMES: Happy Jack, Jumpin' Jack, and Funny Face, as well as the miniatures Jack-Be-Little, Sweetie Pie, and Baby Boo, to name a few. With names like those, these guys are just asking for you to pinch their cheeks. Go ahead, give your guests a Happy Jack to carve or a little Sweetie Pie to decorate.

YOU'LL NEED:
Pumpkins
Pumpkin decorating kits (see page 13)
Newspapers or a plastic tarp
Bowls, for collecting the seeds

PUMPKIN-CARVING TOOLS:
Round hole cutter, for cutting circles
    (available at art supply stores)
Keyhole saw, for cutting neatly through tough
    pumpkin skins
Large spoon, for cleaning out insides
Wood gouges in various sizes, for carving
Linoleum cutter, for cutting grooves and spirals

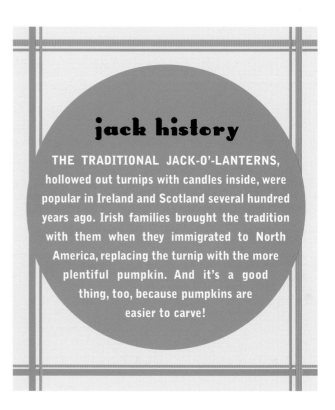

jack history

THE TRADITIONAL JACK-O'-LANTERNS, hollowed out turnips with candles inside, were popular in Ireland and Scotland several hundred years ago. Irish families brought the tradition with them when they immigrated to North America, replacing the turnip with the more plentiful pumpkin. And it's a good thing, too, because pumpkins are easier to carve!

1 Scrub the pumpkins clean with soap and water and let them dry thoroughly.

2 Prepare the work surface by covering it with newspaper or a tarp.

3 Spread out the pumpkin-carving tools, distribute the decorating goody bags and let your guests go to town. Place the bowls nearby so they can put the pumpkin seeds in them for roasting (see page 20).

4 Be sure to display the finished pumpkins so all the other guests can marvel at them.

Trick or Treat!

Trick or Treat!

{THE CENTERPIECE}
self-serve suckers

IT'S SIMPLE AS CAN BE to make this terrific
trick or treat centerpiece.

Power drill
Large pumpkin
Lollipops

Drill holes into the pumpkin, creating a regular pattern, and place the lollipops in
the holes.

cake stands

PRESENT YOUR HALLOWEEN GOODIES ON ONE OF THESE FESTIVE CAKE STANDS—or make several and create a whole display. They look great stacked. Plus, you can easily adapt these stands for use from one holiday to the next by changing the paper and ribbons. All supplies are readily available at crafts and baking supply stores.

pumpkin lore

IT'S A FRUIT, NOT A VEGETABLE! Pumpkins range considerably in size, with some varieties weighing less than a pound, and giant prize-winning pumpkins known to weigh half a ton. They originated in Central America. American colonists invented the pumpkin pie, but their original recipe used the pumpkin as the crust, not the main ingredient: They cut off the pumpkin tops to make handy bowls, which they filled with milk, honey, and spices and then cooked over a hot fire.

YOU'LL NEED:

Decorative paper

Scissors

5-inch Styrofoam round, for base

12-inch foil-covered cake base, for top of stand

Sequin pins

Hot glue gun and glue sticks

2-foot length of 1/2-inch-wide Halloween ribbon

1 Measure and cut a strip of decorative paper to fit around the sides of the Styrofoam base. Measure and cut the paper into a round to fit the top of the cake base.

2 Attach the paper with sequin pins to the Styrofoam and the cake base. Using the hot glue gun, glue the Styrofoam round to the bottom of the cake base.

3 Attach ribbon to the edge of the cake round with sequin pins. For added decoration, cut diamond shapes out of scraps of the decorative paper and attach them with sequin pins to the edge of the cake base underneath the ribbon.

trick or treat

YOUR GUESTS WILL FEEL LIKE KIDS IN A CANDY STORE when you tell them they can eat as much as they want of these delicious goodies.

cupcakes with candy surprise centers

Shh! Don't tell anyone what's hidden inside these delectable cupcakes.

MAKES 12 CUPCAKES

6 cups shredded carrots
   (about 2 pounds)
2 3/4 cups sugar
2 1/2 cups all-purpose flour
2 teaspoons baking powder
1/2 teaspoon baking soda
3/4 teaspoon salt
3/4 cup (1 1/2 sticks) unsalted butter,
   melted and cooled
4 eggs at room temperature, beaten lightly
1/2 cup finely chopped crystallized ginger
   or preserved ginger in syrup, drained
1/4 cup finely chopped dried apricots
1 tablespoon grated fresh ginger
Assorted small candies, for filling cupcakes
Green food coloring
1 container store-bought buttercream frosting
12 small marzipan pumpkins, for garnish (optional)

1 Place the shredded carrots in a strainer over a bowl. Sprinkle with 3/4 cup of the sugar and set aside to drain, stirring occasionally, about 25 minutes.

2 Preheat the oven to 350°F. Grease a muffin tin or line with paper liners.

Sift the flour, baking powder, baking soda, and salt together in a bowl, then repeat twice. Set aside.

3 Using an electric mixer, beat the butter and remaining 2 cups sugar until well blended. Slowly add the eggs and beat well.

4 Gently squeeze the carrots to release as much moisture as possible and discard the liquid. Add the carrots, ginger, apricots, and fresh ginger to the butter mixture and mix at a low speed until blended. Using a rubber spatula, fold in the flour just until moist.

5 Divide the batter evenly in the tins and bake until the cake springs back when touched, about 40 minutes. Remove the cupcakes from the oven and allow them to cool.

6 Carefully cut the top off of each muffin and use an apple corer to make a hole in it. Fill with candy treats and replace the top.

7 Add one or two drops of the green food coloring to the buttercream frosting and mix well. Frost the cupcakes. Top each one with a marzipan pumpkin, if desired.

candy shop bars

This is a handful of a candy-filled treat— how sweet it is!

MAKES 18 BARS

1¹/8 cup (2¹/4 sticks) unsalted butter, softened
1¹/2 cups sugar
2 large eggs
³/4 teaspoon vanilla
3 cups all-purpose flour
³/4 teaspoon baking soda
¹/4 teaspoon salt
10 ounces (1¹/4 cups) crunchy toffee candy bars, chopped

Trick or treat,
you're so neat,
Give me something good to eat.
Nuts and candy, fruit and gum,
I'll go away if you
give me some!

1 Preheat the oven to 350°F. Line a 13-by-9-inch baking pan with greased aluminum foil, letting it hang over the narrow ends of the pan by about 2 inches.

2 Using an electric mixer, beat the butter and sugar until smooth. Beat in the eggs and vanilla. In a medium bowl, combine the flour, baking soda, and salt. Slowly mix the flour mixture into the butter mixture. Add the chopped toffee bars and stir to combine.

3 Scrape the batter into the prepared pan and spread it to the edges. Bake until the top is firm when lightly tapped and a knife inserted into the center comes out slightly moist, 25 to 30 minutes. Let cool completely.

4 Using the excess foil as handles, lift the dessert and transfer it to a cutting board. Carefully peel aw   he foil and cut it into bars.

ice cream witches' hats

Turning the classic ice cream cone upside down makes for a witchy, wonderful treat.

MAKES 10–12 SERVINGS

Colored sprinkles or sugar
10 to 12 sugar cones
1/2 gallon vanilla ice cream or flavor of choice
10 to 12 chocolate dessert shells

1 Pour the sprinkles into a shallow dish and prepare a separate shallow dish filled with water.

2 One at a time, dip the sugar cones into the dish of water, then immediately into the sprinkles. Let dry completely.

3 Place a scoop of ice cream into each of the chocolate cups. Set a sugar cone "hat" on top of each scoop of ice cream.

roasted pumpkin seeds

For the tastiest seeds, scoop out a pumpkin and toast the seeds immediately.

Seeds scooped from 1 pumpkin
2 to 3 tablespoons vegetable oil per cup of seeds
Salt to taste

1 Preheat the oven to 300°F.

2 Rinse the seeds well and pat them dry with a paper towel to remove excess moisture.

3 Toss the seeds with the oil to coat, then spread them in a single layer on a cookie sheet and sprinkle with salt.

4 Bake for 20 to 30 minutes, until seeds are lightly browned and crisp.

hot red wine with cloves and almonds

Nothing takes the chill out of a crisp fall day like a steaming glass of spicy mulled wine.

MAKES 6–8 SERVINGS

1 quart (4 cups) dry red wine
4 ounces (1/2 cup) vodka
4 ounces (1/2 cup) brandy
2 cinnamon sticks
1/2 teaspoon whole cloves
1/2 cup golden raisins
3/4 cup blanched almonds
1/4 cup sugar
1 orange, sliced

1 In a large saucepan, combine all the ingredients. Heat at medium until hot, but do not allow the mixture to boil. Remove the pan from the heat and let it sit for 15 minutes.

2 Return the pan to medium heat and, again, do not let the liquid come to a boil. Pour the mixture through a sieve or strain it into mugs, reserving the orange slices. Serve it garnished with the orange slices.

mulled cinnamon cider

This spicy cool-weather favorite is delicious, whether served with or without a shot of rum.

MAKES 8 SERVINGS

1/2 gallon (8 cups) apple cider
6 cinnamon sticks
1 tablespoon whole cloves
2 tablespoons allspice berries
Zest of 1 orange
Up to 8 ounces (1 cup) rum (optional)

1 In a large saucepan combine the cider, cinnamon sticks, cloves, allspice, and orange zest. Bring the mixture to a boil, then turn the heat down, cover tightly, and simmer for 15 minutes.

2 Strain the mixture into mugs. For guests who prefer the alcoholic version of this beverage, add 1 ounce of rum to the mug.

witches' brew

DISCOVER YOUR INNER WITCH OR WARLOCK!

This easy-to-throw event features pizzas made with ingredients found in a witch's pantry and magical brews to quench the most devilish thirst.

Suitable for sorcerers of all ages, this party works for a small group or a crowd.

hats off!

THESE WITCHY TOPPERS give guests a hint of the fun to come at this hat-trimming event. Be sure to mention any special requests—in this case, beer to drink and scissors to craft with.

GATHER ALL YE WITCHES, WARLOCKS, AND WIZARDS!

WHEN October 31

WHERE 100 Magic Lane (your address and telephone number go here)

BRING Beer, Scissors, Kids

COSTUME Bewitching Basic Black

Pizza Feast! Beer Tasting! Hat Trimming!

RSVP

YOU'LL NEED:
Scissors
8-by-10-inch black cardstock
   (1 sheet for every 2 invitations)
8-by-10-inch orange cardstock
   (1 sheet for every 2 invitations)
Glue stick
Halloween image of your choice
   (Dover clipart images, available at book
   and stationery stores, are a good source)
1/8-inch hole punch
1/4-inch hole punch
8-by-10-inch white cardstock
   (1 sheet for every 2 invitations)
Envelopes to fit the finished invitations

1 From the black cardstock, cut out an oval that's about $4^1/2$ inches long and $1^3/4$ inches high to be the hat brim. Cut out a cone shape that is about 4 inches high and 3 inches wide at the bottom. (It looks nice if the cone shape curves a bit.) Glue the cone piece to center of the hat brim.

2 Cut a $3/4$-by-3-inch strip of orange cardstock. Glue it to the hat to form the hatband.

3 Photocopy an image of a witch using the clipart image of your choice. Cut it out and glue it to the center of the orange band.

4 Use the hole punches to make large and small polka dots from the remaining orange cardstock. Glue them into place to decorate the cone.

5 Type up the invitation on paper so the text will fit the hat shape when cut out. Print it out and glue it to half of the sheet of white cardstock. Trace the shape of the decorated hat piece around the invitation text and cut it out. Repeat until you have as many invitations as you need.

6 Score the text cardstock 1 inch from the tip of the conical hat shape and fold it over a ruler. Apply glue to the cardstock above the crease you have made and press it to the back of the tip of the decorated hat piece.

treat boxes

MAKE THESE CHARMING TRICK-OR-TREAT BOXES IN A TWITCH OF THE NOSE. The gingham checks were inspired by Dorothy's pinafore, but you can use whatever pattern you fancy. Fill the boxes with candy and hand them out to your young guests at the end of the night.

YOU'LL NEED

Scissors

8¹/2-by-11-inch white cardstock (2 sheets per box)

12-by-12-inch scrapbook paper (2 to 3 sheets per box)

Stapler and staples

Glue stick or spray glue

3¹/2-inch diameter round object to use as a template, such as the lid of a jar

Pencil

Scallop-edge craft scissors

Hole punch

Ribbons

1 To make the body of the box, cut a strip of cardstock approximately 3 inches wide by 8 inches long. Cut a strip of scrapbook paper 3 inches wide by 8 inches long, and glue it to the cardstock. Bring the short ends of the strip together to form a large loop, and staple it shut.

2 To make the box bottom and lid, cut a piece of cardstock, 4¹/2 inches by 8¹/2 inches. Cut a piece of scrapbook paper the same size and glue it to the cardstock.

3 Using your round template, trace two circles on the paper-covered cardstock and use the scallop-edge scissors to cut them out.

4 Cut five strips of cardstock about 1 inch long and ¹/2 inch wide. Fold each strip in half.

5 To attach the bottom of the box, place one of the circles paper side up and center the box body on top. Take a strip of cardstock and glue half of the folded strip inside the box body. Glue the other half to the bottom circle. Glue three of remaining strips in the same way, placing them at equal distances from each other.

6 Punch two holes in the top of the second circle and thread ribbon through the holes to make a handle.

optional: Glue half of the last folded strip of cardstock about 1 inch from the edge of the lid. Glue the other half of the strip to the inside of the box to make a hinge.

magical millinery

FIRST LESSON IN "WITCH CRAFTS"? The quintessential witchy hat. Provide your guests with their own hat-trimming kits; tin lunch pails make excellent containers for hat-making materials. Besides scissors, these are the only mortal devices your guests will need to craft their own magical cones of power.

YOU'LL NEED:
Store-bought witch hats
Assorted small feather boas
Craft-store "gems"
Glue
Stackable plastic
    containers
Any other decorations
    that suit your fancy!

Pack a selection of trimmings into each of the boxes and set them out for your guests to pick up when they arrive at the party. Don a hat that you trimmed yourself to chase away inhibitions.

hat-trimming for wee witches

WITCHES ARE SAID TO TRAVEL WITH "FAMILIARS." Although a familiar is typically a black cat or raven, it could certainly take the form of a small child accompanying one of your guests. Here's how to amuse even the littlest witchlet.

YOU'LL NEED:
Orange cone-shaped party hats,
    with a hole punched
        on either side at the edge
        Plastic leis
        Feathers
        Googly eyes
        Paper polka dots
    Ribbons
Glue

1 Don't hesitate to add any fun decoration you can think of to the hat-making table. (Just keep it simple and kid-friendly—no sharp objects, please). Flat-backed items such as buttons or rhinestones that can be glued on work magic.

2 After kids have finished making their hats, tie a ribbon in each of the holes so that they can keep their hats in place, no matter where they decide to fly!

which witch is which?

HALLOWEEN TIC-TAC-TOE: GOOD WITCH VS. BAD WITCH. Make this game pre-party and set up one or more sets on side tables. Tell your guests that it's just like tic-tac-toe: Get three in a row to triumph.

YOU'LL NEED:
Sheet of 12-by-12-inch scrapbook
    paper in mini-checks pattern
Roll of transparent shelf-lining
    paper or book-cover paper
Ruler
Pencil
Roll of 3/4-inch black
    electrical tape
Scissors
Sheet of poster-size black cardstock
Spray glue
2 pictures: one good witch and one bad

6 Photocopy the pictures to make five game pieces of each kind. (Enlarge the images if necessary to make them fit the squares on the game board.) Cut out circles from the remaining cardstock that are the same size as the photocopied pictures. Cut out and glue the copies to the card circles to make the game pieces.

7 Place game sets around the room for your guests to enjoy.

1 Laminate the scrapbook paper with the shelf paper by following the manufacturer's directions.

2 Using the ruler and pencil, divide the paper into three columns, each 4 inches wide. Mark each space, then draw the two vertical lines.

3 Turn the paper 90 degrees and repeat step 2 to form a grid.

4 Place electrical tape over the pencil lines.

5 Cut out a 12 1/2-by-12 1/2-inch piece of the black cardstock. Glue the front of the game board to it.

witchy videos

PLAY THESE MOVIES with the sound muted and you have a spooky visual backdrop for your party.

● *The Witches of Eastwick* (1987) ● *The Nightmare Before Christmas* (1993) ● *I Married a Witch* (1942) ● *Bell, Book and Candle* (1958) ● *The Witches* (1966)

AND A FEW FOR THE YOUNGER CROWD:
● *It's the Great Pumpkin, Charlie Brown* (1966) ● *Escape to Witch Mountain* (1975) ● *The Wizard of Oz* (1939) ● any Harry Potter movie

tempting tidbits

ALWAYS CROWD-PLEASERS, pizza and beer are easy to serve for a small gathering or a large bash. Asking your guests to bring the brew means this party won't break the bank. Be sure to also provide an alcohol-free option such as root beer.

puréed vegetable and pumpkin seed dip

This vegan dip is full of the spirit of autumn.

MAKES 1¹/2 CUPS

1 tablespoon olive oil
1 medium onion, finely chopped
1 clove garlic, crushed (optional)
1 small yellow-fleshed winter squash such as acorn
    or butternut (to make ³/4 cup flesh)
1 medium red bell pepper, seeded and diced
1 teaspoon fresh thyme leaves
¹/4 cup vegetable stock or cold water
2 tablespoons raw pumpkin seeds
Selection of crackers or breads, cut into wedges

1 Heat the olive oil in a sauté pan over medium-high heat. Add onion and garlic and cook gently, stirring occasionally, for 5 minutes, or until tender.

2 Cut the squash in half and scoop out the seeds. Cut the halves into wedges and, using a sharp knife or vegetable peeler, remove the skin. Cut the wedges into small pieces.

the menu

Puréed Vegetable and Pumpkin Seed Dip

Smoky Bacon and Cream Cheese Dip

Crackers and Wedges of Bread for Dipping

Pizza with Pizzazz

Pizzeria-Style Tomato Sauce

Caramelized Onion Topping

Roasted Garlic Topping

Plenty of Brew

Ice Cream Cookie-Witches

3 Add the squash pieces, diced bell pepper, and thyme to the onion mixture and fry for 2 minutes. Add the vegetable stock, bring to a boil, cover, and simmer, stirring occasionally, for 15 minutes, or until the squash is just tender. Allow to cool for at least 10 minutes.

4 Preheat the broiler, then lightly toast the pumpkin seeds. This takes only a few seconds, so watch closely. The seeds will start to make a popping sound when they are ready. Remove them from the broiler and let cool.

5 Place the vegetable mixture and all but 1 tablespoon of the pumpkin seeds into a blender or food processor. Process for a few seconds on a pulse setting if possible. The dip should retain some texture rather than being completely smooth.

6 Transfer the dip to a serving dish and serve warm, or allow it to cool, then cover and refrigerate it. Just before serving the dip, sprinkle it with the remaining pumpkin seeds. Present it with a selection of crackers or bread wedges.

a cauldron of paper napkins

FINGER FOODS DEMAND NAPKINS! And you've got countless choices for decorative Halloween-themed ones—even napkins with screwball cartoon characters. For a minimalist style, choose simple orange and black napkins, then dress them up with a napkin ring made from decorative paper. Just cut the paper into a narrow strip and fasten it into a ring using a glue stick. Tuck lots of these napkin bundles inside a plastic mini cauldron (see page 78 for sources) and let guests help themselves.

smoky bacon and cream cheese dip

To bring out that smoky bacon flavor, chill this dip for at least two hours prior to serving.

MAKES 1$^{1}/_{2}$ CUPS

7 ounces plain cream cheese
$^{1}/_{4}$ cup plain yogurt
2 tablespoons milk
6 ounces smoked bacon slices,
    cooked until crispy then cooled
Freshly ground black pepper
1 tablespoon fresh chives, chopped
Selection of crackers

1 Blend the cream cheese, yogurt, and milk together in a bowl.

2 Crumble the cooked bacon into little pieces. Reserve 1 tablespoon for garnish and stir the remaining bacon into the cream cheese mixture. Season well with freshly ground black pepper. Cover and chill.

3 At party time, spoon the dip into a serving dish and sprinkle it with the chopped chives and reserved crumbled bacon. Serve with crackers.

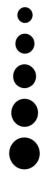

pizza, your way

THIS PARTY PLAN ALLOWS for plenty of improvisation. Here's how to customize the pizza according to your budget and timeframe:

1 QUICK AND EASY: Order in! Ask friends in advance what toppings are their favorites (or just choose a variety of different toppings). Make food flags to identify the options.

2 A LITTLE MORE EFFORT: Order in plain pizzas and provide a selection of toppings such as cheese, olives, and peppers. Here are a few options to consider for added panache: caramelized onions and roasted garlic (see page 32), goat cheese, and nuts such as pistachios.

3 SPEND SOME TIME IN THE KITCHEN: Buy premade pizza crusts, or if you have the desire, and all the necessary tools, go ahead and make your own pizza crusts. This is not very difficult and homemade pizza is sure to please.

pizza with pizzazz

Pizza is a party favorite for sorcerers young and old. Cast a delicious spell on yours by giving the optional toppings witch-worthy names such as Scale of Dragon, Eye of Newt, Wool of Bat, Hearts of Eel, Toe of Frog. To identify the toppings, print out the names on paper, cut out the labels, and glue them to contrasting paper. Attach to a festive swizzle stick, then place it in the center of the topping.

MAKES 6–8 SMALL PIZZAS
(8–10 INCHES IN DIAMETER)

PIZZERIA-STYLE TOMATO SAUCE
One 28-ounce can peeled tomatoes
3 tablespoons extra-virgin olive oil
1 teaspoon minced garlic
3 tablespoons tomato paste
1 tablespoon dried oregano
Salt

6 to 8 premade small pizza crusts (8 to 10 inches in diameter)
Grated cheese, for topping (best-loved pizza cheeses are Parmesan and mozzarella)

SUGGESTED PIZZA TOPPINGS
Pepperoni slices
Sausage, crumbled or sliced
Mushrooms, sliced
Red onions, sliced
Pineapple, cut into small chunks
Red and green bell peppers, sliced
Carmelized onion topping (see page 32)
Roasted garlic topping (see page 32)

1 To make the sauce, strain the juice from the tomatoes into a bowl and set aside. Place the tomatoes on a cutting board, remove the seeds with a spoon, and then chop coarsely. Add the tomatoes to the juice in the bowl and set aside.

2 Heat the olive oil in a skillet over medium heat. Add the garlic and cook, stirring occasionally, until soft but not brown, about 1 minute. Add the tomatoes and juice, tomato paste, oregano, and salt. Bring the sauce to a boil, turn the heat down to a simmer, and simmer, uncovered, stirring occasionally, until thickened, 20 to 30 minutes. Refrigerate for 15 minutes.

3 Transfer the sauce to a food processor and puree until fairly smooth.

4 Top the crusts with the sauce and sprinkle with cheese. Bake according to the package directions.

5 Serve the pizzas hot, along with your selection of toppings.

CARAMELIZED ONION TOPPING

MAKES ENOUGH FOR 6–8 SMALL PIZZAS

1¹/2 pounds white or yellow onions, thinly sliced
2 tablespoons olive oil
Salt and pepper to taste

In a large, heavy pan with a lid, heat the olive oil over medium heat. Add the onions and stir well to coat with the oil. Sprinkle generously with salt and pepper. Cover, reduce the heat to medium-low, and cook, stirring often, until the onions are very tender and well caramelized, about 25 minutes.

ROASTED GARLIC TOPPING

MAKES ENOUGH FOR 6–8 SMALL PIZZAS

3–4 whole garlic heads
Olive oil
Salt to taste

Preheat oven to 350°F. Cut off and discard the top of each garlic head to expose the cloves. Peel away most of the papery outside skin, leaving heads intact. Place the garlic in a baking dish, drizzle with olive oil to coat top surface, and sprinkle with salt. Cover the dish with foil, bake for 30 minutes, then uncover the garlic and continue to cook until soft, 10 to 15 minutes. Remove the garlic from the oven and let cool. Squeeze the cloves into a bowl.

beer: the magical brew

Bewitching beverages for this party should include a variety of autumnal brews. Flavored ales, robust stouts, and seasonal fruit infusions are readily available and make perfect accompaniments to the finger foods on this menu.

Serve the beers in a plastic witch's cauldron (see page 78 for sources) filled with dry ice. Line the cauldron with heavy-duty plastic to prevent leaks, then layer ice alternating with beer bottles. This keeps the beer well stocked and well chilled—and the dry ice adds spooky atmosphere.

Kids can have their own version of witch's brew—it's called root beer.

ice cream cookie-witches

These are simple to prepare, but you will need to allow them some time in the freezer.

MAKES 8 ICE CREAM SANDWICHES

$1/2$ gallon vanilla ice cream or frozen yogurt, softened
16 chocolate chunk cookies
1 cup small chocolate chips
1 cup chopped nuts of choice (walnuts, hazelnuts,
   macadamia nuts are good choices)

1 Line a cookie sheet with foil.

2 Combine the chips and nuts in a small bowl.

3 Spoon about $1/3$ cup ice cream onto a cookie and top it with a second cookie. Press lightly until the ice cream reaches the edges of the sandwich. Repeat with the remaining cookies and ice cream.

4 Roll the side of each sandwich in the chip mixture, pressing lightly to make the chips and nuts adhere. Freeze on cookie sheet until firm, at least 15 minutes.

5 Wrap the ice cream sandwiches in individual freezer bags and place them in the freezer until solidly frozen, about 1 hour. Let them stand a few minutes at room temperature before serving.

it's a mod, mod mod world

IN THE 1960S, LONDON WAS SWINGING, spreading its mod style and high energy to the rest of the world: the Beatles and the Rolling Stones for music, Vidal Sassoon for hair, and Mary Quant for makeup and, of course, the miniskirt. Can't you just hear the music, feel the energy, and see the paisley and the op art? Invite over a dozen or so of your friends, don bodypaint and winklepickers, and party on!

knock, knock

SIMPLE, BUT A REAL KNOCKOUT. Buy as many sheets of card-stock and envelopes as you need to make these groovy invitations for all your guests.

YOU'LL NEED:
Sheets of precut 5-by-7-inch cardstock
Precut 5-by-7-inch window envelopes
Mailing envelopes to fit the window envelopes (check
    with the post office to see if
    additional postage is required)

1 Use your computer to format the text to fit on the cardstock. Print out the words "KNOCK, KNOCK! WHO'S THERE?" on one side of each sheet of cardstock.

2 On the other side of each sheet, print the remaining party details and your answer to the riddle.

3 Slip each sheet into a window envelope with the words "KNOCK, KNOCK! WHO'S THERE?" showing through the window.

KNOCK, KNOCK!
Who's there?
BOO!
Boo who?
YOU'LL BE BOO-HOOING IF YOU MISS
THIS HIP HALLOWEEN SHINDIG!

WHEN October 31
TIME 9 p.m. to ?
WHERE 2 Cool Avenue
(insert your address here)
DRESS Crazy, man!

mod-ify your atmosphere

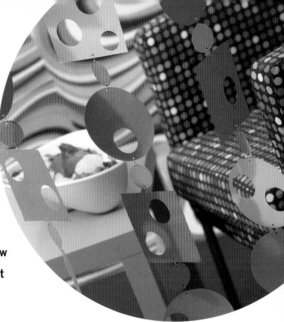

FORTUNATELY, THE LOOK OF THE SIXTIES IS ALIVE and well, with retro style all the rage. It's easy to pick up a few mod accessories at thrift stores, antique stores, and flea markets. If you haven't got time to go hunting for retro treasures, there are brand-new reproduction pieces available, too. Here are some easy ways to retrofit items to transport you back in time.

wall art

ANDY WARHOL'S ART WAS FAR OUT. What he did with a little tinfoil was mind-blowing. Now, with the aid of some simple gift-wrapping items, you too can create mind-blowing art of your own.

YOU'LL NEED:
Low-tack tape (the kind used to mask the molding when you paint walls)
Retro-print wrapping paper

Using the low-tack tape (it won't remove paint from the walls) "wallpaper" as much of the room as you'd like with the wrapping paper. Don't worry if the pattern doesn't match perfectly at the edges—that just makes it op art! Alternatively, put up blank sheets of posterboard and provide water-based poster paints so your guests can create one-of-a-kind wall art! (Clean-up's easy with water-based paints.)

paper room dividers

TO CREATE A FUNKY ATMOSPHERE, hang up some of these temporary walls. Mod, man!

YOU'LL NEED:
Colorful craft paper squares and circles (available at crafts supply stores)
Large hole punch and $1/8$-inch hole punch
S-hooks (available at jewelry supply stores)

Using the large hole punch, punch one or two holes in the paper circles and squares. Save the small circles that you remove from the larger pieces. Using the small hole punch, make holes at the top and bottom of all the paper pieces. String the pieces together with S-hooks, alternating the small paper circles with large circles or squares to make long chains. Hang several chains from the ceiling to create room dividers.

havin' a hullabaloo

COOL, GROOVY, AND FAR OUT are the words for this happening Halloween party.
Get inspired by old movies and television shows (*Alfie* or *Laugh-In*, for example)
or more recent tributes (think *Austin Powers*), and revel in all that was sixties chic.

twist and shout

Think *American Bandstand* circa 1963! The Pony, the
Jerk, the Mashed Potato, and the Locomotion were
a few favorite dance steps of the period. Kids gyrated
to the Twist, a new dance craze created by Chubby
Checker that soon spread to Italy, France, and England.
Play music at this party to inspire these moves—and
matching attitude—on the dance floor.

body and face painting

Spread a little love and happiness by setting up
a face-painting station for your guests. (Face
paints are available at party supply and costume
stores—or use regular makeup.) Famous
icons of the era include the peace sign and
the happy face. Paint them on!

groovy games

Break out those games from yesteryear such
as Twister, Password, and Operation. Laughter
guaranteed!

crazy costumes

Stage a costume show at the party and give out awards
for the most fabulous ensemble. You might want to
preparty with your friends by going shopping together
before the big night. Thrift stores, flea markets, and
your mother's closet are good places to locate some
wild duds.

{THE FOOD}

psychedelic southwestern

SOME LIKE IT HOT! But this dip can be modified—from mild to hot as hell. Go ahead and experiment. Be sure and indicate to your guests which dip is the most powerful.

salsa verde

Salsa, the dip—not the dance!

MAKES 2 CUPS

3/4 pound fresh tomatillos or one 11-ounce can
   whole tomatillos
2 serrano or jalapeño peppers, stems removed
2 cloves garlic, peeled
2 cups packed fresh cilantro
1 medium white onion, coarsely chopped
1/4 teaspoon salt
Tortilla chips

the menu

Salsa Verde

Cranberry-Orange Salsa

Tortilla Chips for Dipping

Santa Fe Corn, Shrimp, and
Black Bean Salad

Shake It Up, Baby! Margarita

Butterscotch Flan

1 If you're using fresh tomatillos, peel off the papery outer skins. Bring a large saucepan of water to a boil and add the tomatillos. Let the water return to a boil, then cook them for 30 seconds and drain immediately. If you're using canned tomatillos, simply drain them.

2 If you want the salsa to be blazing hot, use the whole peppers. Otherwise, cut the peppers in half, then remove and discard the seeds. Mince the garlic and peppers by dropping them through the feed tube of a

food processor while the machine is turned on, or chop them in a blender.

3 Add the tomatillos, cilantro, onion, and salt to the processor or blender. Blend until the tomatillos and onion are chopped. Serve at room temperature with chips.

cranberry-orange salsa

A colorful variation on the classic.

MAKES 1¹/₂ CUPS

2 navel oranges
1 small white onion, quartered
2 cups fresh or frozen cranberries
1 jalapeño pepper, minced
2 tablespoons sugar
¹/₂ teaspoon ground cumin
¹/₄ teaspoon ground cinnamon
¹/₄ teaspoon salt
Tortilla chips

1 Scrub the oranges with a kitchen brush and warm soapy water. Rinse well and pat dry. Cut each orange into 8 wedges.

2 In a food processor or blender, coarsely chop orange wedges and onion by pulsing, add the cranberries, and pulse until all the ingredients are finely chopped.

3 Transfer the mixture to a bowl and add the jalapeño, sugar, cumin, cinnamon, and salt. Mix well. Let sit at room temperature for about 30 minutes to allow the flavors to blend. Serve with chips.

santa fe corn, shrimp, and black bean salad

This flavorful salad pairs nicely with dips and chips.

MAKES 8–10 SERVINGS

1¹/₂ cups dried black beans, soaked overnight
2 cups canned or frozen corn kernels
1 pound large shrimp, shells removed
1 large red bell pepper, seeded and cut into thin strips
3 scallions, thinly sliced
1 cup fresh cilantro

FOR THE DRESSING
1 tablespoon cumin seeds, toasted
¹/₄ cup red wine vinegar
2 tablespoons orange juice
2 teaspoons Dijon mustard
1 teaspoon honey
¹/₂ jalapeño pepper, seeded and chopped
¹/₂ teaspoon salt
³/₄ cup olive oil

1 Drain the beans and put them into a large pot with cold water to cover. Simmer until they are tender, about 45 minutes to 1 hour. Drain and let cool.

2 Cook the corn in salted simmering water for about 3 minutes, drain, and let cool. Cook the shrimp in salted simmering water for about 2 minutes, drain, and let cool.

3 To make the dressing, crush the cumin seeds with a mortar and pestle. Whisk with remaining dressing ingredients in a small bowl until well blended.

4 In a large bowl, toss the beans, corn, bell pepper, scallions, and half of the cilantro leaves with two-thirds of the dressing. In a medium bowl, toss the shrimp with the remaining dressing. Arrange the shrimp over the bean mixture and sprinkle the remaining cilantro leaves over all.

butterscotch flan

Since these delectable individual desserts are served chilled, they can be prepared ahead of time.

MAKES 8 SERVINGS

FOR THE CARAMEL
1/2 cup water
3/4 cup sugar
Pinch of cream of tartar

FOR THE FLAN
4 eggs
4 egg yolks
3 cups whole milk
1 cup dark brown sugar, firmly packed

1 To make the caramel, pour 1/4 cup of the water into a heavy, medium-sized skillet or saucepan, and sprinkle the sugar over it in an even layer. Cook over medium heat, adding the cream of tartar when the sugar has dissolved. Do not stir at any time.

2 As the sugar begins to brown, watch it carefully. When the caramel has turned a dark reddish-brown and begins to smoke, remove the pan from the heat and quickly add the remaining 1/4 cup water. Stir to make sure the caramel has completely dissolved.

3 Pour about 1 tablespoon of the hot caramel into each of 8 individual 4-ounce ramekins or ovenproof custard cups. Allow the caramel to harden.

4 Meanwhile, make the flan: Briefly whip together the eggs and the egg yolks in a mixing bowl. Heat the milk in a saucepan over medium heat.

5 When the milk is warm, pour it into the egg mixture, whisking constantly to prevent the eggs from cooking. Add the brown sugar and whisk to dissolve. Strain the custard into a large measuring cup.

6 Preheat the oven to 350°F. Pour the custard into the caramelized ramekins or custard cups. Put the custard cups into a deep ovenproof pan and fill the pan with warm water until it reaches halfway up the sides of the custard cups. Cover tightly with aluminum foil and bake for 35 to 45 minutes, until the custard is barely set in the middle but firm around the edges. Remove the baked custards from the water and set them aside to cool. Refrigerate until ready to serve.

7 To unmold, run a sharp knife around the outside of each chilled custard. Invert a serving plate over the custard and flip. Shake a few times to release. Pour the remaining caramel from the ramekin over the flan.

shake it up, baby!
margarita

Coarse salt

**1 jigger (1$\frac{1}{2}$ ounces)
good-quality tequila**

$\frac{1}{2}$ ounce Triple Sec or Cointreau

Juice of $\frac{1}{2}$ lime

Lime wedge, for garnish

1 Moisten the rim of a glass, then dip it in the coarse salt. **2** To make a shaken margarita, shake the tequila, Triple Sec, and lime juice together with ice. Strain the margarita into the glass and garnish with a lime wedge. **3** To make a blended margarita, combine the liquors and lime juice with 4 to 6 ice cubes in a blender and blend until the ice is almost but not quite disintegrated. Pour the margarita into a glass and garnish with a lime wedge.

tip:

You might find that margaritas are too popular to make one by one! Make a whole pitcher of them by multiplying out the number of people you want the batch to serve. So, for 6 guests you need 6 jiggers of tequila, 3 ounces of Triple Sec, and 3 ounces of lime juice.

hocus
pocus

ABRACADABRA IS THE PASSWORD TO THIS SPELLBINDING PARTY.

Bubbles from Champagne cocktails will cast a spell

on your guests at this intimate gathering for four. Charms and potions

allow guests to make their own magic, then dip into the bubbling

fondue-pot cauldron for a delectable dinner among the stars.

{THE INVITATION}

let the magic flow!

WARNING: Casting spells can be a risky enterprise. But so is missing this party! This event is all about conjuring, so let that be your inspiration when you conjure up the invitations. Print out your distinctive message onto silver cardstock, glue on a silvery moon, then send it into the universe.

YOU'LL NEED:
Precut silver cardstock
Paper silver moon decorations (available at craft and stationery stores)
Envelopes to fit the cardstock

1 Using your computer, type up your message in a magical font. Print out your text directly onto silver cardstock to make one invitation for each guest.

2 Glue a silvery moon onto each invitation, slip them into envelopes, and send them to your lucky guests.

Boil and bubble,
Toil and trouble,
To you warts and nose hair
If you miss this affair!

PARTY That magical night, October 31
TIME 8 P.M. to ?
PLACE 100 Magic Street
(insert your address here)
COSTUME Dress to bring out
the sorcerer in you!

{THE DECOR}

table of enchantments

HOLD YOUR GUESTS SPELLBOUND with this elegant table setting. Silver chargers topped with frosty white dinner plates create a fascinating full-moon effect.

YOU'LL NEED:

Sparkly metallic tablecloth (such as silver lamé)
Silver cardboard stars in assorted sizes
   (available at party supply stores)
Colorful glass marbles or clear crystal balls
White tea lights
White beads
Star-shaped candleholders

Drape the table with the cloth and scatter silver cardboard stars around it, using larger ones as placemats and smaller ones as coasters. Hang medium-sized stars from the ceiling, so they dangle overhead. Set star-shaped name cards (see right) at each place setting and artfully arrange colorful glass marbles or clear crystal balls on the table for a mystical feel. Place a few white beads in the bottom of each candleholder and nestle white tea lights in the beads.

starry place cards

MAKE THESE LUMINOUS PLACE CARDS in a twinkle of the eye.

YOU'LL NEED:
Small- to medium-sized silver cardboard
   stars (available at party supply stores)
Alphabet rubber stamps
Silver inkpad
Clear embossing powder
Heat gun
Stand-up memo clips

Spread newspaper over your work area to protect the surface. Choose a star the right size for the name you need to put on it and stamp the first letter of the name near the left edge. Sprinkle embossing powder over the wet ink, then dry it with the heat gun. Repeat until the name is spelled out completely. Center the star in a memo clip on a dinner plate so your guest can find his or her place with ease.

charm balls

UNRAVEL THE ORB TO SEE WHAT'S IN STORE FOR YOU! Styrofoam balls wrapped in crepe paper strips with tiny charms and fortunes tucked inside are sure to enchant. You can make unique fortunes by typing out wishes on paper then cutting them into little strips. Here's your chance to deliver some holiday cheer—customize the fortunes to suit your guests' desires.

YOU'LL NEED:
Roll of white crepe paper
4-inch Styrofoam balls
Box of sequin pins
Assorted small charms, fortunes, Swedish
    fortune-telling fish
Assorted ribbons of various widths,
    1 yard of at least 2 kinds of ribbon per ball
Paper silver moon ornaments
    (available at craft and stationery stores)
White glue

1 Unwind the roll of crepe paper about 12 inches. Secure one end to a Styrofoam ball with a sequin pin.

2 Wind the crepe paper over and around the ball, tucking in charms, paper fortunes, and the fortune-telling fish as you go. When you have inserted all the charms and fortunes, wrap the crepe paper a few more times to finish off the ball and secure the loose end of the crepe paper with a second sequin pin.

3 Tie two or three different ribbons around the ball. Glue a silver moon to the knot (and if you have customized the fortunes to a particular guest, write that person's name on the moon).

spellbinding spell book

NEED A LITTLE HELP FROM THE COSMOS to bring luck and love? A Spell Book can be mighty useful and oh-so-easy to make. Why not slip a potions recipe into each one and give these little beauties to your guests? That way they'll have everything they need when it comes time to make do-it-yourself potions at the party (see Potion Power, page 50). Don't have time to create individual spell books? Just print out a sheaf of potions recipes in a Gothic font and pass around to your guests.

YOU'LL NEED:
Sheet of decorative paper
Sheets of plain paper
Scissors
Small pads of blank paper
Stapler and staples
Ruler
Rubber cement or paper glue
8$1/2$-by-11-inch silver cardstock or sparkly paper
Sparkly cording
Calligraphy pen or marker
Decorative labels
Gems in star shapes

1 Type up a title page for the spell book and print it out on the decorative paper.

2 Type up the potion recipes (see pages 50 and 51) and print them out on the plain paper, formatting the text so that it will fit on sheets the same size as the notepads. Make one copy of each recipe per spell book.

3 Cut the pages with the spells printed on them to the same size as the notepad. Cut the decorative title page

to fit the paper pad, adding an extra $1/8$ inch near the top of the paper. Score the paper so that you can fold that $1/8$ -inch strip over a ruler.

4 Neatly staple the four pages with the spells on them behind the title page with the spells facing forward. Place the staples just below the fold in the decorative paper. Dab the folded strip of decorative paper with glue and attach it to the top of the notepad.

5 Cut the silver cardstock to fit over the front, back, and top of the notepad, adding $1/4$ inch to the length. Glue the cardstock to the back of the pad, score it so that you can fold it over the top, and then glue it down to the top and front so that the extra $1/4$ inch of cardstock extends off the front of the pad. Score that flap and fold it so that it fits around the bottom of the pad.

6 Write "Spells" on a decorative label and affix the label to the front of the book, threading sparkly cord underneath the label as you attach it.

7 Finish the book by gluing a star-shaped gem to the label. Instruct guests to take their spell books to the potion-making table to make their own potions.

potion power

IF WANT ADS AND PERSONALS AREN'T WORKING, encourage guests to take matters into their own hands with a little do-it-yourself potion-making. A few incantations can't hurt—who knows? They may work miracles. Color is fantastically symbolic, so encourage everyone to match the right envelope to the potion. And don't forget to have guests check in a week later to report on the results!

YOU'LL NEED:
Potion ingredients, listed opposite
Mortar and pestle
Red, orange, white, and green envelopes
Blank labels (available at stationery stores)
Pens

1 Place all the necessary ingredients in bowls, making sure to label the bowls to identify what is inside, and arrange them on a large table. Provide a mortar and pestle for grinding the ingredients together.

2 Have guests put together their potions, following the instructions in their spell books. If you prefer, instead of having guests handwrite their own labels, you can print them out ahead of time on the computer.

endless love

Combine the following ingredients in a red envelope labeled *love powder*: sprinkle over bedsheets nightly for one week.

3 pinches of yarrow
3 pinches of lavender
2 pinches of rose petals
1 pinch of ground ginger

JUST FOR FUN: heart-shaped confetti and a key (as in the key to your heart!)

good luck

Combine the following ingredients in an orange envelope labeled *luck powder*: **sprinkle in your shoes to bring positive changes into your life.**

2 pinches of vetiver
2 pinches of ground allspice
1 pinch of ground nutmeg
1 pinch of calamus

JUST FOR FUN: a horseshoe charm, star-shaped confetti (for wishing on!), and a lucky penny

fabulous wealth

Combine the following ingredients in a green envelope labeled *wealth powder*: **sprinkle in your wallet or purse.**

2 pinches of cedar shavings
2 pinches of patchouli
1 pinch of galangal
1 pinch of ground ginger

JUST FOR FUN: play money

to your health

Combine the following ingredients in a white envelope labeled *health powder*: **for protective energy, sprinkle in a circle and stand within it.**

2 pinches of eucalyptus
1 pinch of myrrh
1 pinch of thyme
1 pinch of allspice

JUST FOR FUN: a Band-Aid, green tea bags, and star-shaped confetti

the power of red

RED IS A POWERFUL COLOR, associated with luck, protection, passion, and warning. The Pennsylvania Dutch drew red lines around their barns to keep out witches. A gift of red roses means "I love you." In China, lucky red envelopes containing money are traditional New Year gifts.

a magical repast

FONDUE IS A FRENCH TERM THAT MEANS "MELTED." Though not your typical Halloween party food, it's the perfect dish for this party, because it resembles a bubbling cauldron. Offer up some magic-wand breadsticks and phenomenally gooey taffy apples to go with the fondue and your guests will think you're a sorcerer.

the menu

Cider and Cheese Fondue

Breadsticks with Prosciutto and Robiola

Heavenly Champagne Cocktail

Warm Taffy Apples with Cinnamon Twists

cider and cheese fondue

Boil and bubble! The apple cider provides a seasonal twist.

MAKES 4 GENEROUS SERVINGS

12 ounces Gruyère cheese, finely grated
1 clove garlic, crushed
1 cup plus 1 tablespoon medium-dry
   apple cider
1 tablespoon cornstarch
Freshly ground black pepper
Apple wedges, cubes of
   crusty bread, chunks
   of cooked ham, rolled
   slices of prosciutto,
   tomato edges, and
   asparagus spears,
   for dipping

1 Place the cheese, garlic, and 1 cup of the cider in a heavy-bottomed saucepan and heat gently until the cheese has melted completely into the cider, about 20 minutes.

2 When the cheese has melted, blend the cornstarch with the remaining cider in a small bowl. Stir in 2 tablespoons of the hot fondue mixture. Immediately pour the cornstarch mixture into the pan and stir well. Season well with pepper.

3 Pour the fondue into a warmed fondue pot or heatproof serving dish. Keep it warm over a fondue burner, table-top warmer with tea lights, or a hotplate. Serve with the dipping accompaniments.

breadsticks with prosciutto and robiola

This is an edible version of a magic wand. With the heavenly flavor of robiola, a savory but mild cream cheese, and the smokiness of prosciutto, these breadsticks will all but disappear into thin air.

MAKES 15 BREADSTICKS

4 ounces robiola
15 crunchy breadsticks, at least 5 inches in length
8 pieces thinly sliced prosciutto
15 chives, left whole

1 Spread a thin layer of robiola on each breadstick.

2 Cut each slice of prosciutto in half. Wrap a strip around each breadstick.

3 Tie each breadstick with a chive to finish.

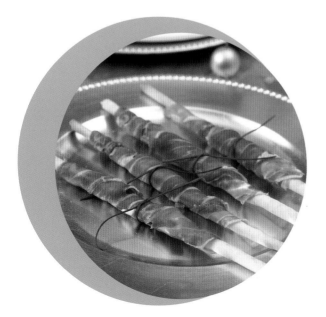

foolproof fondue

FONDUE CAN BE FINICKY. Here's how to keep things simmering:

1 Before using your fondue pot for the first time, read the manufacturer's instructions closely and always take care when handling the pot if it's filled with hot liquid.

2 Always choose a dry wine or cider and use a strong-flavored cheese. Don't worry if at first the cheese separates from the wine; just keep stirring—it will gradually become smooth and creamy.

3 Melt the cheese slowly. Do not let it boil or it will become stringy. If it begins to boil, lower the heat, stir, and continue to cook gently until the mixture becomes smooth.

4 If the cheese curdles, add a teaspoon of lemon juice and beat well.

warm taffy apples with cinnamon twists

The apples, twists, and sauce can all be made in advance. Simply rewarm the apples and sauce before assembling the serving dish. Be warned, though, the apples will perform a disappearing act as they cook— so start with the largest apples you can find.

MAKES 6 SERVINGS

FOR THE APPLES

6 large Granny Smith Apples
3/4 cup (1 1/2 sticks) unsalted butter
1 1/2 cups sugar
3 tablespoons brandy
1 tablespoon fresh lemon juice

FOR THE PASTRY TWISTS

1/2 sheet frozen puff pastry
2 tablespoons unsalted butter, melted
1/4 cup sugar
1 teaspoon ground cinnamon

FOR THE TAFFY SAUCE

2 1/2 cups sugar
1/2 cup water
1 cup heavy cream
1/4 cup coarsely chopped peanuts

heavenly champagne cocktail

Bliss in a flute.

MAKES 1 COCKTAIL

1 small sugar cube
Angostura bitters
Chilled Champagne

1 Place the sugar cube into a champagne flute and drip 1 or 2 drops bitters over it.

2 Fill the glass with Champagne.

1 To prepare the apples, peel and core them, leaving them whole. Cut off the tops and bottoms to make flat surfaces for the apples to rest on.

2 Melt the butter in a medium skillet over medium heat. Stir in the sugar and cook over medium-high heat, stirring until the mixture begins to turn golden brown and to caramelize. Add the brandy and lemon juice and stir to blend. Adjust the heat so that the mixture remains at a simmer.

3 Place the apples in a single layer in the liquid and simmer until the submerged portion is tender, basting occasionally, about 15 minutes. Turn the apples over and cook them until they're tender all the way through, about 15 minutes more. Remove them from the liquid and set them aside to cool.

4 To make the twists, preheat the oven to 400°F. Line a sheet pan with parchment or buttered wax paper.

5 Unroll the puff pastry on a work surface and brush it with melted butter. Toss the sugar and cinnamon together and sprinkle the mixture evenly over the pastry. Working lengthwise, cut the pastry into 6 long strips, each 3/4 inch wide. Lightly twist the strips, keeping the cinnamon sugar on the inside, to make long twisted straws with barber-pole stripes of plain and cinnamon-sprinkled pastry. The finished straws should be about 8 inches long.

6 Transfer the straws to the prepared pan, run your fingers along them to straighten them, and bake for approximately 20 minutes, until puffed and golden brown.

7 To make the sauce, pour the sugar into the center of a saucepan. Carefully pour the water around the sugar, trying not to splash any sugar onto the sides of the pan. Do not stir; gently draw your finger through the center of the sugar, making an X, to moisten it. Cook, without stirring, until the mixture is light caramel in color. Immediately remove it from the heat.

8 Carefully stir in the cream with a wooden spoon until smooth. (Be careful: It will bubble up and may splatter.)

9 To serve, place the apples on a serving dish, drizzle them with caramel sauce, sprinkle them with peanuts, and place a pastry straw in the hole of each apple so it resembles a wooden stick.

haunted house

YOUR HOUSE MAY NOT BE A MODERN-DAY VERSION OF THE MUNSTERS' EERIE ABODE, but there are fast and easy ways to "creep" it up for a Halloween brunch of otherworldly proportions. Set a fascinating table full of spiders, bats, and ghosts sure to delight guests of all ages. Play scary music or stories on tape. Lower the blinds and draw the drapes. Keep lots of lit candles going, even during daylight. Twine spiderwebs over the furniture. You'll be surprised at how effectively this rouses ghosts and goblins from their hiding places!

{THE INVITATION}

eerie open house

THIS INVITATION WILL QUITE NATURALLY FLY through the mail. Made from purchased notepads in the shapes of ghosts and bats (see page 78 for sources), these are as easy to put together as one-two-three. This treatment can also be adapted for party décor.

It's creepy and kooky,
but most of all
it's spooooooooooooky!

PLACE 9 Ghoul Lane
(insert your address here)
DATE October 31
TIME High noon
COSTUME Dress like Casper!

YOU'LL NEED:
Notepad in the shape of ghosts
Notepad in the shape of bats
1/8-inch hole punch
S-hooks (available at jewelry supply stores)
Calligraphy pen or marker
Envelopes to fit the finished invitations

1 Tear off two pages from each of the notepads. Using the hole punch, make holes on both the left and right sides of one of the ghosts and one of the bats. Make a hole on the right side of the remaining ghost page, and make a hole on the left side of the remaining bat page.

2 Attach the pages together with S-hooks to form a chain, alternating the ghosts and bats.

3 In nice penmanship, print the text on the invitation, dividing the information up among the four pages in the way you like best.

4 Fold up the pages and place them in the envelope.

spidery piñatas

KEEP LITTLE GHOULS BUSY with these easy-to-whip-together piñatas.
They'll be a sure hit at this spook-a-rama.

YOU'LL NEED:
Scissors
Black crepe paper
Small-sized paper bag
Newspaper
Transparent tape
Candy, trinkets, and toys
1 yard ribbon
1/4-inch hole punch
Orange craft paper
Glue stick
4 black pipe cleaners
Stapler or hot glue gun

1 Cut a length of black crepe paper double the size of the paper bag. Place some crumpled newspaper in bottom of bag to hold it in the proper shape.

2 Set the paper bag in the middle of the crepe paper. Bring up the ends of the paper to cover the front and back of the bag. Fold and tape the sides shut. Fill the bag with goodies, then tie it closed with ribbon.

3 Using the hole punch and the orange paper, punch out two small circles and glue them to the center near the top of the bag to look like spider's eyes. Fold the pipe cleaners in half and attach these "legs" underneath the spider with a stapler or hot glue gun.

scary noises

Howl-o-ween! **THIS IS A GREAT ACTIVITY FOR KIDS.**
Teach them how to record these easy-to-make sounds using a cassette recorder with a looping cassette in it, so the sounds will play over and over.

• **RAIN:** Spray water from the sink sprayer into a bowl or turn on the shower and let the water fall into a bucket.

• **WIND:** Heat a teapot full of water until it whistles or blow across the top of an empty glass or plastic bottle.

• **FIRE:** Crumple an empty potato chip bag.

• **FOOTSTEPS:** Fill a shallow pan with uncooked rice and walk in place in the box. Start slowly and build up speed.

• **THUNDER:** Rattle a large sheet of posterboard.

4 Hang the piñata from the ceiling (in an open area where there's nothing fragile around!). Let kids whack at the piñata with a stick until it breaks open and releases the goodies.

shhh!
spirits lurking

An eerie tradition known as "the Dumb Supper" was brought to America from Africa. During dinner on Hallomas (that's Halloween to us) nobody is allowed to speak, not even in a whisper, since this encourages the spirits to come to the table.

a boo-tiful table!

CREATE A SPINE-CHILLING ATMOSPHERE that any spook would admire. For a realistic dungeon look, position a faux rock wall (they're available from theater supply shops) behind your dining table. Then go for the creepiest, crawliest table setting you can manage.

YOU'LL NEED:
Silver tablecloth
Black, sparkly tulle
Plastic spiders
Tree branches
Raven ornaments (available at party supply stores)
Spiderweb (available at party supply stores)
Sparkly sand
Brandy snifters
Tea lights

Drape the table with the silver cloth and layer the black tulle over it. Attach some plastic spiders by threading their legs through the holes in the tulle. Then, create a center-piece using the branches, ravens, spider-webs, and more plastic spiders. Pour some sparkly sand into the brandy snifters and place the tea lights in the sand.

batty napkin rings

THEY'RE DREADFUL! So simple to make, and so spooky.

Scissors
Purple netting
Black sparkly twine
Package bat picks (paper bat ornaments attached to wires)
Black napkins

Cut a piece of purple netting long enough wrap around a folded napkin. Tie it shut in back with a small length of sparkly twine. Gather 3 or 4 bat picks in a bundle and tie them together with the twine. Attach them to the purple netting on top of the napkin.

dungeon chic

• **IF A ROCK WALL ISN'T IN YOUR BUDGET,** buy sheets of Styrofoam and textured-finish spray-paint. It's available at craft supply stores in many different stone-look colors.

• **BLACK LIGHT PAINT** glows in the dark when exposed to a black light bulb, contributing to the already eerie environment.

jeepers creepers

YOU MAY NEVER HAVE GIVEN (OR EVEN ATTENDED) a Halloween brunch, but this fanciful menu might make you a convert.

sausage ghoulash

This hearty melange will give your guests strength to face the ghastly sights and sounds of your haunted house.

MAKES 4 SERVINGS

2 orange bell peppers
2 to 3 large Yukon Gold potatoes (1$^3/_4$ pounds)
2 tablespoons butter
1 to 2 tablespoons olive oil
1 clove garlic, peeled and minced
Salt and freshly ground pepper
1$^1/_4$ pounds spicy chicken or Italian pork sausages
12 to 16 pitted black olives
1 tablespoon chopped chives
Juice of $^1/_2$ lemon

1 Preheat the broiler. Place the peppers on a foil-lined baking tray and broil them, turning them until the skin blackens. When charred, place peppers in a paper bag or in a bowl covered with plastic wrap. Let them cool until you can easily peel away the skin. Rinse the peppers, remove the stems and seeds, and cut each one into 4 or 5 slices.

2 Peel the potatoes, halve them lengthwise, and cut them into slices. Pat dry. Heat the butter and 1 tablespoon of the olive oil in a large skillet. Add the potatoes and sauté them over medium heat until golden, 15 to 20 minutes. When they are nearly done, add garlic and salt and pepper to taste. Turn off the heat.

3 Meanwhile, in a separate skillet, sauté the chicken sausages in the remaining tablespoon of olive oil over medium-low heat. (If you are using pork sausages, sauté them with 2 to 3 tablespoons water over medium-low heat.) When the sausages are browned and cooked through, drain them and cut into $^1/_2$-inch slices.

4 Add the peppers and sausage to the potatoes and heat the mixture through. Stir in the olives and chives. Add lemon juice to taste.

bacon and egg salad

This salad makes use of traditional breakfast staples.

MAKES 4 SERVINGS

1/2 pound mixed baby salad greens
1/2 cup halved and pitted kalamata olives
2 large ripe tomatoes, seeded and diced
4 slices bacon, cooked crisp and crumbled
1/2 cup olive oil
3 tablespoons white wine vinegar
1 teaspoon Dijon mustard
1/4 teaspoon salt
1/4 teaspoon coarse-ground black pepper
4 large eggs
Clover or alfalfa sprouts, for garnish

1 Divide the salad greens among four plates. Gently toss together the olives, tomatoes, and bacon. In another bowl, whisk together the oil, 2 tablespoons of the vinegar, the mustard, salt, and pepper.

2 Fill a medium skillet with water, add the remaining tablespoon of vinegar, and bring the water to a gentle boil. Crack the eggs into the water and poach them, about 3 minutes. Using a slotted spoon, place eggs on the greens. Spoon the tomato mixture on top and drizzle with vinaigrette. Top with sprouts and serve immediately.

sweet potato and black pepper biscuits

These sweet and spicy biscuits are so good it's scary.

MAKES 10 BISCUITS

1 1/4 pounds sweet potatoes
3 tablespoons orange juice
3 tablespoons unsalted butter, melted
1 1/2 cups all-purpose flour
1 tablespoon baking powder
1 teaspoon sugar
1/2 teaspoon baking soda
1/2 teaspoon salt
1/8 teaspoon ground cloves
1/8 teaspoon coarse-ground black pepper

1 Preheat the oven to 400°F. Lightly grease a 9-by-9-inch baking pan or a baking sheet.

2 Place the sweet potatoes on the pan and bake for 1 1/4 hours, until very soft. Cool, peel, and mash enough pulp to equal 1 cup.

3 In a medium bowl, stir the sweet potatoes, orange juice, and butter together until well combined. Add the flour, baking powder, sugar, salt, cloves, and pepper. Knead the mixture in the bowl until a soft dough forms.

4 Turn the dough out onto a well-floured surface and knead until smooth. Pat the dough out to a circle about 6 inches in diameter and 1/2 inch thick. Cut out eight biscuits with a 2-inch cutter dipped in flour. Gather the scraps, pat out again, and cut two more biscuits.

5 Place the biscuits, barely touching one another, on the prepared pan and bake for 15 to 20 minutes, until the bottoms are lightly browned.

orange biscotti dipped in chocolate

The aroma of oranges, the sweetness of milk chocolate, and the crunch of the biscotti—what could be more delectable?

MAKES 4 COOKIES

**4 store-bought orange biscotti
1 bar (approximately 1¹/₂ ounces) milk chocolate
Halloween-themed decorative baking candy**

1 In a small saucepan over medium heat, melt the chocolate, stirring occasionally and watching it carefully to prevent burning.

2 Line a cookie sheet with wax paper and set it aside. Pour the candy into a small, shallow dish.

3 Dip the biscotti in the melted chocolate, then swirl them in the candy. Place the biscotti on the prepared cookie sheet and allow the chocolate to harden. Serve with coffee and tea.

bloody mary

Even Dracula would approve of this tangy recipe.

MAKES 1 COCKTAIL

**1 jigger (1¹/₂ ounces) vodka
6 ounces (³/₄ cup, or 4 jiggers) tomato juice
2 or 3 drops fresh lemon juice
2 or 3 drops Worcestershire sauce
1 drop hot red pepper sauce
Pinch of celery salt
Pinch of salt
Pinch of ground black pepper**

Shake all the ingredients together well with ice, then strain the cocktail into an ice-filled glass.

creepy bites for kids

Kids can be finicky eaters, so you'll want to make your menu as uncomplicated as possible. Here are a few fun ways to creep them out and get them to eat.

 GHASTLY GRUEL: Serve up a variety of cereals and call them fanciful phantom names such as Post Ghosties or Kellogg's Frosted Frights.

 TERRIFYING TOASTIES: Using a ghost-shaped cookie cutter (and other Halloween shapes), cut sliced bread into creepy shapes. Toast lightly and serve with butter and blood-red jam.

LITTLE GHOST PEEPS: Thread a Ghost Peeps marshmallow candy onto a straw and place it in a glass of milk.

the ghouls vs the ghosts

Ghouls are evil spirits with coarse gray hair and long sharp fingernails, best known for their grave-robbing tendencies. Ghosts aren't necessarily evil: They're the victims of an untimely death who must return to the scene of the tragedy again and again. How can they be released? If they get to tell their sad story to a sympathetic listener.

that
old devil
moon

WHEN IT'S FULL, THE MOON PLAYS ALL MANNER OF DEVILISH TRICKS,

so tonight, whatever happens, just blame it on the moon. Supernatural events,

daredevil antics, pranks, and all kinds of mischief and mystery are allowed.

At this spirited party, your guests will watch as the cards are turned to reveal

past, present, and future. They'll marvel at the answers that the Magic 8 Ball

grants. They'll even make their own fortune-telling device. The recipes are simple and

can be completed well in advance—perfect for a larger number of revelers.

Go ahead, ask everyone you know!

spin the wheel of fortune

THIS PARTY GETS A LOT OF ITS REVELATIONS FROM THE MAGIC 8 BALL.
So we borrowed a few phrases for this witty invite.

I SEE
A party in your future
Tonight is the night
Luck is on your side
It is undoubtedly so

YOU'LL NEED:
Magic 8 Ball clipart or other clipart of choice
    (check out Dover clipart images,
    available at book and stationery stores)
Paper fasteners
2 sheets yellow paper
2 sheets red paper
6-by-9-inch piece of scrap paper
Calligraphy pen or marker
6-by-9-inch plastic envelopes

1 Using your computer, format each phrase to print on a separate piece of colored paper. Arrange the clipart image of your choice below one of the phrases. Print two of the phrases on red paper and two on yellow.

2 Fold the piece of scrap paper diagonally, so that there is a crease running from the top right corner to the bottom left. Then unfold it and fold on the other diagonal. The creases on the paper should now divide the paper into four triangles. Using these triangles as templates, cut the printed yellow paper and red paper each into two triangles, with the phrases at the outer edges, as shown in the photo.

3 Arrange the triangles into a rectangle, alternating red and yellow pieces of paper, and photocopy them in color, making as many as you need.

4 Cut arrow shapes from the remaining pieces of yellow paper and attach each in the center of an invitation, using a paper fastener.

5 Print the party information on the back of each invitation.

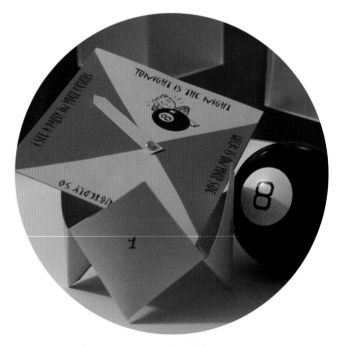

paper fortune-teller

IT'S IN YOUR HANDS! TO SUMMON UP COURAGE, accomplish any task, or answer life's questions, you may need a little assistance. Take charge of your own fate with this handy homemade fortune-teller, which you may remember from grade school. Put together a few of these clever divination tools (shown at left in yellow, to match the invite) and leave them out for your guests to enjoy—or enlist someone to sit at a table and read your guests' fates.

YOU'LL NEED:
1 sheet 12-by-12-inch yellow cardstock
Markers in assorted colors

1 Fold each corner of the cardstock into the center.

2 Turn the square over and fold each corner to the center one more time.

3 Number the segments visible on the paper 1 through 8. Fold up the flaps of paper and write a different fortune under each number. Need a few suggestions?

- You'll have a devil of a good time
- It's undoubtedly so
- Someone is waiting for you
- Tonight is the night
- Ask again
- The answer is yes

3 Turn the square over and use the markers to make each of the four quadrants a different color. Fold the piece in half one way and then the other. Push the flaps up and place your thumb and index finger on each hand under the flaps.

4 To use the fortune-teller, have a person pick one of the four colors. Spell that color out, saying each letter as you open the fortune-teller first one way, then the other. Stop and have the person pick one of the visible numbers. Open and close the fortune teller, first one way, then the other, as you count up to that number. Have the person choose a flap and then fold it up to reveal the fortune.

{THE DECOR}
create a supernatural setting

THIS EVENING SHOULD RESONATE WITH WISDOM and insight. Set up small tables and chairs so that partygoers can move easily from one divining station to the next. Set a Magic 8 Ball on one table, tarot cards on another, and a paper fortune-teller on another. Shroud each station in secrecy by hanging lush red curtains. For added intrigue, hire a professional psychic or palm reader for the evening.

the art of fortune-telling

The position of the stars, the appearance of comets in the sky, the fall of the dice, and many other techniques all belong under the general heading of the mantic, or prophetic, arts. Some of the most popular methods are the tarot, cartomancy (reading playing cards), palmistry, and numerology. At this party, focus on the tarot. Most packs come with instructions, and many books are available for additional help.

tarot basics

Even though there's disagreement about its actual origins, most people believe the tarot began in Egypt. The most popular deck in use today is the Marseilles pack, which was developed in the late fifteenth century to simplify the method and provide greater ease of interpretation. Another popular deck is the Rider-Waite, developed in 1910 by A. E. Waite. Tarot decks consist of seventy-eight cards—twenty-two major arcana and fifty-six minor arcana. The major arcana are trump cards adorned with illustrations that symbolize the journey through life, showing the setbacks and opportunities a person meets along the way. The minor arcana are numbered cards similar to playing cards.

shop around

If you're uncertain about your abilities to remember the meanings of all seventy-eight cards at once, buy a pack with illustrations on the numbered cards of the minor arcana. These will help you to remember their basic meanings and provide clues for subtle interpretations.

Practice a few times on yourself, then when the big night arrives, thrill your friends with predictions for their futures.

giving a reading

Sit opposite your guest and ask him or her to shuffle the cards while thinking about a question. Then ask the guest to cut the deck three times with the left hand and reassemble the pack in a different order. The cards are now ready to be revealed and should be dealt off the top of the pack. Ask the guest to give you a general idea of the question. Decide which "spread" (instructions for this will be included with your pack) to use and deal the cards accordingly. Always choose your words carefully when interpreting the cards. Remember, this is for fun. You don't want to send anyone home in tears!

the devil made me do it

THESE SPICY TEMPTATIONS ARE SO DIABOLICALLY GOOD, your guests would sell their souls to get just one more.

deviled eggs

You might just think of these piquant eggs as a summer picnic staple, but they're devilishly good at a Halloween bash, too.

MAKES 24 PIECES

12 hard-boiled eggs, peeled
1/4 cup mayonnaise
1 tablespoon Dijon mustard
Salt and freshly ground black pepper
1/4 cup chopped chives, for garnish
   (optional)

1 Cut the hard-boiled eggs in half and arrange the whites on a serving platter. Place the yolks into a small bowl.

2 Add the mayonnaise, mustard, and salt and freshly ground pepper to taste to the yolks. Stir until well combined.

3 Spoon the yolk mixture into the indentations in the egg whites and garnish with fresh chives if desired.

deviled chicken wings

You might say these chicken wings have ESP—for "extra spicy poultry," that is.

MAKES ABOUT 24 PIECES

2 tablespoons vegetable oil
$1/2$ cup honey
3 tablespoons whole-grain mustard
2 tablespoons Dijon mustard
1 tablespoon cider vinegar
$2/3$ cup dry unseasoned breadcrumbs
1 teaspoon dried thyme
$1/2$ teaspoon ground red pepper, or more
  to taste
$1^{1}/2$ pounds chicken wings
  (about 24 wings)

1 Preheat the oven to 400°F. Grease a large baking sheet with the vegetable oil. In a large bowl, combine the honey, mustards, and vinegar. Stir until smooth.

2 On a plate, combine the breadcrumbs, thyme, and ground red pepper.

3 Cut off and discard the chicken wing tips. Separate each wing into two pieces at the joint; trim excess fat and skin. Toss the wings in the honey mixture. Place the wings one at a time into the crumb mixture and turn to coat completely, shaking off the excess.

4 Arrange the wings on the prepared baking sheet. Bake, turning the wings with tongs twice during cooking, for 20 to 30 minutes, until they are well browned and crispy. Serve hot or at room temperature.

31st cocktail

Numerology, anyone? Brighten up your outlook with this delightful, fruity variation on a martini.

MAKES 1 COCKTAIL

1 ounce vodka
1 ounce cherry brandy
2 teaspoons dry vermouth
1 tablespoon orange juice

Shake all the ingredients together with ice, then strain the cocktail into a martini glass.

hellfire punch

There's nothing like punch to liven up a party—but who says you need a traditional punch bowl? Choose a container that suits your fancy and fill it with this festive punch.

MAKES 12 SERVINGS

10 cups cranberry juice cocktail, plus more for ice
    cubes
3 cups orange juice
1 cup fresh lime juice
Vodka, rum, or tequila to taste
Sugar to taste (optional)

Combine all the ingredients, including the alcohol of your choice, in a large punch bowl. Mix well and adjust the sugar to taste. For more brilliant color, add ice cubes made from additional cranberry juice.

magical marzipan cake

You may not be a cake-making queen, but you can bake a simple cake-mix cake and dress it up in marzipan to look royally beautiful. Marzipan, or sweetened almond paste, is available at local supermarkets. You'll need about a pound of it to cover an 8-inch-square cake. To prepare it for rolling and cutting, knead it well.

TO CREATE MARBLED MARZIPAN

1 You will need a bottle of food coloring in the color of your choice. Start by rolling out the marzipan onto a surface sprinkled with confectioners' sugar and working it into a thick sausage shape.

2 Use a toothpick to apply the food coloring in thin stripes along the marzipan roll. Fold the marzipan over and over again into a thick sausage shape. Keep rolling

and folding until it is streaked with color, adding dots of additional food coloring if necessary.

3 Roll out the marzipan and apply it to the cake as described below.

TO COVER THE CAKE

1 Apricot jam is used to help keep the marzipan in place, and it doesn't affect the flavor of the cake. Heat up a jar of jam and strain it through a sieve. Brush the syrup on the surface of the cake.

2 Sprinkle a little confectioners' sugar on a flat work surface. Roll out the marzipan with the rolling pin into a thin sheet large enough to drape over the cake. Use the rolling pin to help support the rolled-out sheet of marzipan so that it doesn't crack while you lift it and place it over the cake.

3 Use your hands to press the paste onto the surface of the cake, starting at the top and smoothing down the sides. Remove excess marzipan from the corners of the cake and around the base with a sharp knife.

TO MAKE NEAT SQUARE CORNERS

1 Alternatively, you can cover the sides and top of the cake with separate pieces of marzipan. Brush melted, strained jam on top of the cake and roll out a thin sheet of marzipan that it is about 1 inch larger all around than the top of the cake. Turn the cake upside down and center it over the marzipan, then trim the marzipan around the line of cake. You can also cut a decorative edge in the marzipan, if you'd like.

2 Spread jam around sides of cake and cut strips of marzipan to fit. Press the strips onto the cake and use your fingers to smooth over the joins.

{THE SOURCES}

Every year there are more and more creative Halloween party and craft supplies to choose from. Below are sources for the items featured in this book, along with some other essential stores to visit (both online and off) for all your Halloween needs.

Witches' Brew: Page 22: Lamps from Ikea. Black cat swizzle sticks from Reminiscence. Pages 24 and 25: Table from Ikea. Page 26: Wizard of Oz lunch pails from Vandor/The Lyon Company, *www.lyonco.com*. Beads and gems from Magic Scraps. Page 29: Plastic Cauldron from Party City.
Tricks and Treats: Page 8: Paper Lanterns from Seasons of Cannon Falls. Page 16: Paper on cake stands from Midori. Cupcakes from Cheryl Kleinman, Baker, 718-237-2272. Page 12: Pumpkin-carving kit from Restoration Hardware. Whimsy ribbons on bag from Midori. Page 15: Pumpkin sucker from Sheryl's Chocolate Creations, 1-888-882-2462, *www.sherylschocolate.com*. **It's a Mod, Mod World:** Page 38: Parson's table and chairs and chair covers from Ikea. Memo holder from Crate and Barrel. Cardstock and envelopes from Paper Access. Page 39: Serving dish from Crate and Barrel. Wrapping paper from Reminiscence. Page 40: Luncheon tray from Target. **Hocus Pocus:** Page 44: Table, chairs, and chair covers from Ikea. Fondue pot from Crate and Barrel. Page 46: Table from Ikea. Silver cardstock and envelopes from Kate's Paperie. Page 50: Vellum envelopes from Kate's Paperie. Herbs and spices from Aphrodisia, 264 Bleecker Street, New York, NY 11014, 212-989-6440.

Gems from Magic Scraps. **Haunted House:** Page 56: Table and chairs from Ikea. Ravens from Seasons of Cannon Falls. Page 58: Ghost- and bat-shaped notepads, Party City. Page 59: "Boo" ribbon from Midori. Page 61: Bat charms from Seasons of Cannon Falls. Purple Coastal Netting from Magic Scraps. Page 65: Ghost placemats from Target. Frankenstein doll from Seasons of Cannon Falls. **That Old Devil Moon:** Pages 68 and 77: Cake from Cheryl Kleinman, Baker, 718-237-2272. Page 70: Magic 8-Ball from Target. Page 73: Table, chairs, and chair pads from Ikea. Page 74: Serving dish from Crate and Barrel. Page 76: Cocktail shaker from Crate and Barrel.

ABRACADABRA SUPERSTORE
19 West 21st Street
New York, NY 10010
212-627-5194
Visit *www.abracadabrasuperstore.com* to shop online.
Costumes, wigs, masks, makeup, magic, and more!

CRATE AND BARREL
Visit *www.crateandbarrel.com* to locate a store near you.
This houseware chain carries party tableware and other festive props.

DOVER PUBLICATIONS
Visit *www.doverpublications.com* or call 516-294-7000 for a retail outlet near you.
A fun and easy source for holiday clipart.

GOODWILL
Visit *http://locator.goodwill.org/* to locate a store near you.
A classic source for thrifty costumes, tableware, and more.

HALLOWEEN MAGAZINE
www.halloweenmagazine.com
An online magazine dedicated to all things Halloween.

IKEA
Visit *www.ikea.com* to shop online or checkout the locations of warehouse stores.
For festive and affordable furnishings and decorative accessories.

JOANN FABRICS
Visit *www.joann.com* to shop online or call 800-525-4951 to locate a store near you.
A nationwide chain specializing in arts and crafts supplies, including costume patterns, decorations, and more.

KATE'S PAPERIE
561 Broadway
New York, NY 10012
212-941-9816
Visit *www.katespaperie.com* to shop
online.
This upscale stationery store carries a
dazzling selection of paper supplies to
inspire your holiday crafting.

LILLIAN VERNON
Call 800-901-9291 for a catalog
or visit *www.lilianvernon.com* to
shop online.
At holiday time, this company carries
a wide assortment of decorations and
costumes for Halloween.

MAGIC SCRAPS
www.magicscraps.com
A fabulous source for crafting supplies,
tips, and techniques. Designers are available if you need specific crafting advice.

MARTHA STEWART ONLINE
www.marthastewart.com
During the holiday season, this website
offers lots of products and inspiration for
making Halloween decorations, snacks,
and costumes.

MICHAEL'S ARTS AND CRAFTS
Call 1-800-MICHAELS or visit
www.michaels.com to locate a store
near you.
This arts and crafts chainstore offers
everything you'll need to make your
holiday crafts.

MIDORI
708 Sixth Avenue North
Seattle, WA 98109
206-282-3595
Visit *www.midoriribbon.com* to shop
online.
Unique arts and crafts supplies.

PAPER ACCESS
www.paperaccess.com
This online retailer sells stationery and
other festive notions.

PARTY CITY
Visit *www.partycity.com* to locate a
store near you.
Stores nationwide carry a huge selection
of Halloween party gear, tableware, and
costumes.

REMINISCENCE
50 West 23rd Street
New York, NY 10001
212-243-2292
Visit *www.reminiscence.com/index.html*
to shop online.
Vintage clothing, fashionable accessories,
and groovy collectibles.

RICKY'S
Visit *www.rickys-nyc.com* to shop
online.
A wide selection of wigs, costumes, props,
accessories, and makeup. Order from the
website or visit the stores in New York
City and Florida.

RESTORATION HARDWARE
Visit *www.restorationhardware.com*
to locate a store near you.
For stylish, vintage-inspired housewares
and decorating ideas.

SEASONS OF CANNON FALLS
Visit *www.seasonsofcannonfalls.com*
or call 1-800-776-2075 for a retail
outlet near you.
For creative, often hand-crafted notions
for your home.

SPENCER'S
Visit *www.spencergifts.com* to locate
a store near you.
With stores nationwide, Spencer's is
a good place to find blacklights, props,
toys, and other Halloween oddities.

SPIRIT HALLOWEEN SUPERSTORES
Call 1-800-COSTUME or visit
www.spirithalloween.com to locate
a store near you.
Shop online or visit one of the temporary
locations open for business from
September 1 to November 1 in major
metropolitan markets nationwide.
Supplier of party goods, decorations,
costumes, accessories, masks, wigs, and
makeup.

TARGET
Visit *www.target.com* to locate a store
near you.
A wide selection of affordable adult
and children's costumes, decorations,
tableware, and candy.

{THE INDEX}